Sh*tty Jobs

The Guide to Surviving a Recession

John LaLoggia

NEWMAN SPRINGS PUBLISHING
320 Broad Street
Red Bank, NJ 07701

First originally published by Newman
Springs Publishing 2021

ISBN 978-1-63692-676-6 (Paperback)
ISBN 978-1-63692-677-3 (Digital)

Printed in the United States of America

Introduction

George: I like sports. I could do something in sports.

Jerry: Uh-huh. Uh-huh. In what capacity?

George: You know, like the general manager of a baseball team or something.

Jerry: Yeah. Well, that—that could be tough to get.

George: Well, it doesn't even have to be the general manager. Maybe I could be like, an announcer. Like a color man. You know how I always make those interesting comments during the game.

Jerry: Yeah. Yeah. You make good comments.

George: What about that?

Jerry: Well, they tend to give those jobs to ex-ball-players and people that are, you know, in broadcasting.

George: Well, that's really not fair.

Jerry: I know. Well, okay. Okay. What else do you like?

George: Movies. I like to watch movies.

Jerry: Yeah. Yeah.

George: Do they pay people to watch movies?

Jerry: Projectionists.

George: That's true.

Jerry: But you gotta know how to work the projector.

George: Right. Okay. Sports, movies, what about a talk show host?

Jerry: Talk show host. That's good.

George: I think I'd be good at that. I talk to people all the time. Someone even told me once they thought I'd be a good talk show host.

Jerry: Really?

George: Yeah. A couple of people. I don't get that, though. Where do you start?

Jerry: Well, that's where it gets tricky.

George: You can't just walk into a building and say "I wanna be a talk show host."

Jerry: I wouldn't think so.

George: It's all politics.

Jerry: All right, okay. Sports, movies, talk show host. What else?

George: This could have been a huge mistake.

—*Seinfeld*, season 2, episode 7

Work

*God would never let me be successful. He'd
kill me first. He'd never let me be happy.*

YOU'RE NOT ALONE—WORK sucks. We have to do it
for a decent life. Some people like their job, but I'll
bet there are far more people that would rather be
doing something else.

Obligation kills inspiration. Jimmy Kimmel
said, "If it's on the calendar, I don't want to do it."
And he loves his job.

You will always have to work in some capacity,
and for many of us, it will be something we don't
love. The purpose of this book is to help you get
through your shitty job and/or unpleasant job search.

My wife, who works in the hospitality industry,
was extremely successful at a very young age rising
up the ranks of the corporate world. Her view is that,

regardless of the job, a person should try to be the best they can. To which I say, ideally, sure; but the reality is they don't. They might have the necessary skills to be good at their job, but it's a constant struggle day after day to put forth the effort to be successful because they don't love it or don't care.

There seem to be two options. One, you can quell your passion as the singular focus in your life and take the "work to live" motto. Provide for your family. Have a nice life enjoying vacations and good meals. Your passion becomes your hobby. Conversely, you can relentlessly pursue your passion even through these demeaning, disheartening jobs.

You have to choose the best path for yourself. I've done both. I worked at jobs I've hated, and I've also had jobs I liked. What I found is I worked harder and put forth infinitely more effort into jobs I wasn't paid for and liked versus jobs I was paid for and hated. Those roles should be reversed, but they aren't. My two passions in life are sports and comedy, so when I did internships at ESPN Radio 1000 and Comcast SportsNet in Chicago, I killed myself because I wanted to work at those establishments. I was an intern at two different improv comedy theaters, and I didn't mind taking out the trash if it meant being able to learn how to perform and write comedy from some of the best comedy teachers in the world. I labored over the things I cared about versus things I didn't. People rarely lose their jobs for things they care deeply about unless, you know, a generational global pandemic hits.

I graduated college in 2009 right as the 2008 recession was coming into play. I'm fully aware that the unemployment rate of 2008 wasn't nearly as bad as the recession due to COVID-19, but the same recession strategies apply. If it feels like you were dealt a bad hand, you were. It's okay to be upset. This fucking sucks! Venting aside, the recession happened to everyone, not just you. The point of this book is to help you through it.

- Your situation is temporary. Remind yourself of this. Cynicism is easy and self-defeating. It is much harder to try. Embrace the chaos. Record unemployment, racial injustice, environmental collapse, and a pandemic. Acknowledge it and use it to build your roadmap forward.
- Be fearless. Don't stop putting yourself out there. It will pay off. As I write this, I keep getting email notifications about jobs I applied for that I didn't get. Job search

tip number one, when the email starts with "unfortunately," you can delete it.

- Endure the journey. When someone tells me to "enjoy the journey," I want to drop-kick them because we're not all taking the same journey. Some of us are traveling in private planes while some of us are roller-blading. Not all journeys are enjoyable. A journey is change, and change is hard. Navigating through a recession is hard. You have self-doubt, anxiety about the world, and a rapidly diminishing bank account. Breathe through the bullshit. That's your therapy session for today. My fee is $5,000. (Give me a break. I'm unemployed). I'm currently looking for jobs because I was laid off due to COVID-19. Luckily for me and other millennials, this is not our first recession. For those of you who have never been unemployed or have done a job search during a recession, fear not. Millennials know it all too well and can help you through this ridiculous time. We can provide you with strategies on how to detect fake companies, dealing with emotionally unstable recruiters, and what it's like moving back in with your parents.

- Laugh at yourself. This is quite a predicament you find yourself in. Twenty percent of the country is unemployed, and you're trying to find a job. This premise is technically funny according to comedy doctrine. You may not think so right now, but in a few years, you'll be laughing your ass off about your time during quarantine and how ridiculous some of your jobs have been during the recession. The best way to get through these shitty jobs is to laugh at yourself. Laugh at your situation, coworkers, low pay, boss, commute—all of it. If I didn't laugh my way through all of the strange twists and turns that have gotten me where I am today (unemployed and eating pizza Pringles from the can), I would've fallen into despair and may have given up. I wanted to so many times. I felt like everything I did was wrong for several years and seriously considered invoking the George Costanza model of doing the opposite of everything until things started to turn around. My worst jobs created some of my most interesting and memorable experiences now—not at the time.

- You're not alone. Allow the following—very real—stories to illustrate this and, hopefully, make you feel better.

Gummy Worms

Jerry (looking at George's textbook): Risk management?

George: Yeah. Steinbrenner wants everyone in the front office to give a lecture in their area of business expertise.

Jerry: What makes them think you're a risk management expert?

George: I guess it's on my résumé.

DURING THE SUMMER of 2008 between my junior and senior year of college, I got a job as a bartender at a local restaurant where people "eat good in the neighborhood." I'd like to think I was hired for my excellent interviewing skills, but it was mainly because I had reliable transportation and a pulse.

I initially interviewed for a server job, but what I really wanted was to be a host. The host was by far the most appealing. I had a new captive audience for my jokes. I only had to converse for two minutes tops, and most importantly, no risk of physical labor (minimal physical output). Why on earth would I want to be a server running around the restaurant all night? For tips? No, thanks. I wasn't in this job for the money; I was in it so my mom wouldn't bother me about getting a summer job. I discussed the host position with the hiring manager who said, "We usually give that job to teenage girls." She asked me if had ever bartended before, and I said, "All the time." The truth was not only had I never bartended before, but I barely drank alcohol. I had also just turned twenty-one, so "all the time" meant I met the legal drinking age for about two weeks. I want to be clear that, during the entire time I was a bartender, I did not know how to make any drinks. I mean ANY drinks. The way I made drinks for customers was to look at a picture of the drink from our menu and, based solely on the mixture of colors, discern the correct type of alcohol for the drink. For example, because of the brown coloring of a Long Island ice tea, I would consistently pour anything I could find that looked like it would go in that drink—e.g., brandy, whiskey, Sprite, orange juice, and, obviously, ice tea. My dad, a nose-to-the-grindstone businessman, couldn't understand why I couldn't take the time to study the book and learn the drinks to be better prepared. Well, Dad, I didn't have fifteen minutes to sit and read which type of liquors go in which drink; and if the customer saw me looking at the booklet, it wouldn't inspire much confidence. But if they didn't know then, they would soon figure it out upon receiving their drink. The 98.9 percent of mixed cocktails I made for customers all came back with the same response: "This doesn't taste right."

My problem wasn't just with mixed drinks; it was with all alcohol. At the time, I didn't know there was a difference between red and white wine. I didn't know which one was cold and which one isn't. I'm still not sure. I worked the graveyard shift which was Monday to Friday, 11:00 a.m. to 5:00 p.m. There were never more than ten customers during that time, and the two types of customers who were at the bar consisted of infidel coworkers and alcoholics.

The only way a customer of mine was going to get their correct drink was to order a bottled beer. I say bottled because, if they ordered something on draft, I didn't know how to fix the tap if beer ran out. As a result, many customers received frothy white foam in their frosted beer mugs. Changing the keg entailed an elaborate maze of going down the basement, moving heavy beer kegs, and sifting through hundreds of plastic tubes, trying to sync up the right beer keg. A host would never have to do that. Because of my limitations as a bartender, I would push bottled beer on customers 100 percent of the time regardless of their order. A woman once asked for a dry martini with a twist of lemon and three olives.

"How about a nice Miller Lite in a bottle?" I said.

Now you are probably thinking, *John, weren't customers upset with you*? Absolutely! All the time. In fact, regulars stopped coming to the bar and started asking for a table. I would wave at them from the bar. To be fair, this restaurant was on its last leg. It wasn't making money, and management would often lament about the low volume of customers. The restaurant closed within six months after I left to go back to college, probably for employing people like me. We had servers selling psychedelic mushrooms and weed behind the restaurant in the to-go parking lot on the regular. I think they generated more revenue than the restaurant during that time.

As the summer continued, kids would occasionally come in with their parents for lunch. This happened maybe three times during my stint as a mixologist. The Dirt Shake, a popular dessert on the kid's menu, was a vanilla shake with Oreo crumbles topped with gummy worms. This was one of the few drinks I could actually make. We had all the ingredients at the bar, so I didn't have to move which was a plus. They had an industrial-size, five-pound bag of gummy worms behind the bar which was only to be used for the Dirt Shakes.

There are certain things people binge eat—chips, crackers, etc. I struggle with gummies. Not just worms, any type of gummy candy. Bears or worms, it doesn't matter. I cannot stop eating them. We weren't allowed junk food in my house growing up, so because I was deprived of such deliciousness, I developed a severe binge-eating problem with gummies. It started with just one and then three, and before I knew it, I had eaten a quarter of the bag. No problem. I'm an adult; I can stop myself. I'll just wrap up the bag and put it away. I relax for a bit, serve a couple of bottles of beer, and then have lunch. An hour goes by, and I can still see the bag on the counter behind the bar. So I have a couple more. After a while, I noticed that I had eaten half the bag, and suddenly my stomach started to hurt. I rolled up the bag and shoved it in one of the lower drawers under the bar so I wouldn't be tempted. Out of sight, out of mind. After a few more hours, my shift ended, and I went home. The next day, about an hour in, I looked for the gummy worms; and I remembered I'd put them in the bottom drawer under the bar. I laughed at how ridiculous this was and reminded myself that I'm not a child without self-control. I don't need to hide a bag of gummy worms to not eat them. I have the willpower to put them back on the counter. So I grabbed them from the bottom drawer and moved them up on the counter. About twenty minutes later, I finished the entire bag.

The next day, I came in, and the hiring manager asked to see me in her office. She asked me why the inventory for the gummy worms was so low.

I promptly said, "I don't understand."

After all, I wasn't the only bartender who worked there. Maybe the night bartender was sneaking some too. Or maybe she was too busy making proper drinks for customers.

She said, "John, I know you've been eating them."

I doubled down and said, "Huh?"

She then queued up surveillance tape from the bar of me scarfing down a five-pound bag of gummy worms at warp speed.

I said, "Oh yeah, those are for the Dirt Shakes."

She said, "They are supposed to be for children."

I felt ashamed, but she didn't realize that I had been deprived of these treats my entire life. Maybe if I explained that to her, she might start to understand why I did what I did.

"Hillary, I didn't get gummy worms growing up, so it's hard for me to stop eating them. But I know I can stop."

She replied, "Okay, John, I've never had this conversation with an employee before. Just remember, they are for kids."

The following Monday when I came into work, I set my stuff down, put on my bartender's apron, and started cleaning the bar. While I was cleaning, I noticed that they had purchased a new five-pound bag of gummy worms. A wave of relief came over me as I saw the bag had not been opened. It was a different brand which meant that the manager went out to buy it herself from a nearby store as opposed to ordering and waiting days for it to ship. I had learned my lesson from the previous week, so I was laser focused on solely making disgusting drinks for customers. However, these gummy worms were sour and coated with sugar. I never had those before. But there wouldn't be any temptation because the bag hadn't been opened yet. As luck would have it, my third customer of the day was a mom along with her three-year-old daughter. She asked for a diet coke (thank God), and her daughter wanted a Dirt Shake.

I replied, "A regular vanilla shake is actually better than a Dirt Shake."

The mother said, "No. She wants that Dirt Shake with crumbles and worms on top."

I began making the shake until, finally at the end, I had to open the new bag. I opened it and put a couple of worms on top and served it to the little girl. They finished their drinks and left shortly after that. At that point, I didn't try to fight anymore as I grabbed a handful of gummies and kept going. The top layer of my tongue was dissolving from the sour-sugar coating, but I didn't care. This went on for hours until I had eaten about three-fourths of the bag. I felt like I had blacked out like an alcoholic who thought he only had a few drinks but actually had twenty. I shoved the bag in the bottom drawer again and counted the minutes until my shift was over.

When I came in the next day, I was, again, called to my manager's office. You'd think, at this point, I'd be reprimanded for being a bartender who didn't know how to make drinks; yet sitting on her office desk was the rolled-up bag of gummies. I could tell she wasn't happy because the first words out of her mouth were "What the fuck is wrong with you!"

What happened next is something I still cannot comprehend. Being summoned not once but twice to your boss's office because you couldn't stop eating gummy worms that were meant for children would be problematic and embarrassing for most people. But just then, a calm came over me that put me in a relaxed state. It was a reminder that I didn't even like this job; in fact, I hated it. The whole restaurant was a joke. Their main revenue source was back-alley drug dealing, and I only had three weeks left until I went back to college.

I said, "I'm really sorry about this, but I cannot stop eating these gummy worms. So you can either fire me, make me a host, or just let me finish out the next three weeks. But I'm not going to stop eating them."

I understandably assumed I would be fired on the spot, so as I started undoing my apron, my manager replied, "Ugh, just go back behind the bar. I'm taking the gummy worms during your shift. If people ask for Dirt Shakes, just tell them we're out."

I couldn't believe what happened. It felt like being on trial where I was clearly guilty for not doing any work but got acquitted because the prosecutor also did not want to do any work. My manager was just as apathetic about her job as I was about mine.

Neither of us cared about what we were doing, but we had to show up every day and appear like we did. If you're reading this and saying to yourself, *I disagree because I love what I do and get excited about showing up every day*, that's great! I'm so happy for you, but this book isn't for you. It's for us.

Hobby, Job, or Career?

*You know I always wanted to pretend
that I was an architect.*

AFTER I GRADUATED college, I did improv and
sketch comedy in Chicago all through my twenties. I studied at places like the Second City, iO, and
the Annoyance Theater. I had the best time of my
life and made some of my best friends. For years, I
spent almost every night out either performing or
watching comedy. I was always a huge comedy nerd,
so I became completely obsessed with improv culture—hanging out drinking at the bar after the show,
unsuccessfully trying comedy bits to impress other
female improvisers, and just thinking about comedy
twenty-four seven. Because it's not New York City
or Los Angeles, your chances to get a job or career
in comedy in Chicago are limited. The best you

could hope for is to get on either the mainstage at Second City or do well in an iO showcase for a once-a-year *SNL* audition. A comedy writer for the *Colbert Report* once said he thought about teaching a comedy class in Chicago called "There Are Other Jobs Than *SNL*." I fully jumped into everything I could: sketch writing, improv, musical improv, and, occasionally, stand-up. I loved doing all different forms of comedy, but after several years, I realized it resulted in great pleasure but no money. In fact, you lose a tremendous amount of money doing improv by paying for classes and force other people to lose money by coming to your terrible shows. It's a little like a pyramid scheme. There are virtually no jobs for professional improvisers because it's not a career. The most successful improvisers in the world made their careers in writing, acting, and becoming TV showrunners. Improv was just a hobby, not a career. Whether your hobbies are playing video games or golf, they will always be hobbies unless you are truly exceptional. If you're not, that's okay; call it a hobby. It infuriates me that I'm okay at a variety of things but not exceptional at any one thing. The goal is to figure out how to leverage your hobby into a job so you can build a career. You might not get exactly what you want right away; a job is the purgatory between a hobby and a career.

If you're having difficulty deciphering between a hobby, job, or career, I created a cheat sheet.

John's work equation

Excitement + work = hobby

No excitement + work + talent (sometimes not) = job

Excitement + work + talent = career

My jobs have been in marketing for the last ten years. One of the annoying things about a job is you are forced to utilize your talent that should be reserved for your career. You almost want to explain to your boss, "I'm sorry, I think there's been a mistake. I know you think I'm a marketing manager, but I'm really an actor." You obviously can't say that, but that's how a lot of people who have jobs feel. It is important to ration your talent, especially if you're at a job you don't like. You'll need to use a little of it to do good work but not too much. Your shitty job deserves a modicum of your talent which should be coveted and cultivated in the direction of a career that means something to you.

I finally got my first real job with actual responsibilities at age twenty-seven. That job pulled me out of the chaos, and for the first time, things started to slow down to where I was able to start taking control of my life. It was a full-time position at a market research company that offered a base salary, benefits, and a 401(k), which was a shift from my previous jobs where I had been compensated in discarded food and sweatshirts.

I didn't love this job, but it offered me enough value to make an effort. Most of the jobs I had during the dark times (we'll get to these) didn't earn my full effort because they didn't fully value me and they were terrible. Remember, just because you're not at your dream job, that doesn't mean you can't experience joy while you're there.

One of our clients was a condom company. They were testing out new products. We had a contest amongst our staff for who could come up with the raunchiest, most inappropriate idea names for the different types of descriptions.

I won.

Idea	New Product Idea Description	Condom Aspect	Possible Names
1	A condom that is scientifically developed to increase the sensation both inside and out thanks to a roomy, stimulating pouch and internal ribs to intensify the pleasure of both.	shape	Gushers
2	A condom that has a patented antibacterial coating that helps prevent natural bacteria buildup, cleans, and sterilizes during intercourse. It does it with specially formulated all-natural ingredients that have no side effects.	lubes/ ingredient	Mr. Peen

3	A condom integrated with a pleasure ring that is super stretchy for a pleasurable fit around the base of the penis. This combined technology will provide the safety benefits of a condom while also maximizing the hardness for longer and intensify the pleasure of both.	device +	Ring Poppers
4	A condom that is coated with a patented formula which will help gain and maintain an erection and intensify the pleasure of both.	health	$E=Pv^2$

5	A condom made from a new patented synthetic material which is thinner and stronger than a typical latex condom. Because it's not made from latex, it is safe to use for people with latex allergies. Also because the condom is thinner, you feel closer to sex than regular latex condoms.	material	Latexual Healing
6	A condom with a patented combination of ingredients which are designed to increase blood flow to the penis which contributes to your maximum size to intensify her pleasure.	lubes/ ingredient	Combo Splatter

7	A condom integrated with a ring that provides vibration to stimulate the clitoris. It is specially designed with material that is comfortable to wear while also maximizing the hardness for longer and intensifies the pleasure of both.	device +	Forever Hung
8	A condom that contains a combination of plant-based ingredients that help stimulate the nerve endings to increase sexual pleasure.	lubes / ingredient	Mother Girth
9	A condom uses a new patented technology with a high water content, making it uniquely soft and supple. Just like your skin, it molds to your individual shape and reacts to your body heat, providing just the right level of lubrication.	material	H-2-Blow

10	A condom that has a technology at the base of the condom that is able to measure and track a range of "performance" parameters and communicate with your smartphone via an app. The condom is thin and flexible. It feels like a second skin and has deeper ribs along the whole condom to increase stimulation for both partners.	device +	iBone
11	A condom made from a new patented synthetic material which is designed to replicate the vaginal wall internally and the penis externally so it more closely replicates the feel of sex without a condom for both partners, providing the closest feel to natural sex with a condom.	material	The Great Wall of Vagina

12	A condom that contains moving beads that can be felt by both partners for increased stimulation during sex and intensifies the pleasure of both.	shape	Just Bead It
13	A condom that is coated with a special lubricant which will stimulate the vaginal muscles to contract during sex so both partners will have a closer, more pleasurable sex experience.	health	LubeTube
14	A condom that contains a reservoir tip that is designed to specifically target the female G-spot, adding additional pleasure for her to achieve orgasm in a way that is not possible without this condom.	shape	Reservoir Hogs

In my two years of working at that company, winning this contest meant more to me than anything else I had accomplished prior. Take note of the aspects of your job that give you joy. They can act as a compass on where to put your time and effort going forward.

Fake Jobs

*Every decision I've ever made in my
entire life has been wrong. My life is the
opposite of everything I want it to be.*

ONE OF THE most important things to remember
when searching for jobs in a recession is to be aware
of fake companies. The more desperate you become
for a job, the more fake companies you'll find. What
is a fake company? A fake company is technically a
real company but with misleading job descriptions
that in no way fully explain the role or accurately
depict what the company does. Many of these took
advantage of sites like Indeed and LinkedIn—a
step-up from roadside signs offering 100k a year to
"be your own boss."

   Shortly after I graduated college and was living
at home with my parents, I got a response on Indeed

for a marketing job from a company called Sports Marketing Inc. I was a sports broadcasting major in college, so I was excited to get a response from a company that was in my field of study (kind of). The job description was "Performing marketing duties for the Major League Baseball team Chicago White Sox." Who better to market for the White Sox than an actual baseball fan? Mark Buehrle might even appreciate some of my analysis on his cut fastball when we hung out at corporate events, or General Manager Kenny Williams and I could discuss strategy at team meetings.

I was ecstatic that I would have the opportunity to get to work for an MLB team—right out of college! I immediately responded and said that I would be interested in learning more about the opportunity. They got back to me and explained the next step was an in-person interview. A normal company usually administers an initial phone screen call before an in-person interview to verify you're not insane before they welcome you into their office. In my case, I assumed they were impressed with my sports broadcasting undergrad degree from a college they had never heard of and clearly wanted to fast-track me.

Their office wasn't at the White Sox ballpark as I previously thought. It was in Aurora, Illinois, a suburb fifty minutes outside of Chicago. I pulled up to their nondescript building which was dark brown with three small trees that were recently planted out front. I was dressed in a full suit and tie for my interview. I had prepared a few marketing and social media strategies for the White Sox that would help bring more fans to their game. I walked into the building to start my future in sports marketing.

They escorted me to a room that was set up in a half circle of chairs centered around a TV. There were about fifteen chairs with different people sitting in them. After a few minutes of silence, I leaned over the woman next to me and asked what she was interviewing for. Ironically, everyone waiting in the room was applying for the same position I was. An employee of the company walked in and put on a movie for all of us to watch while we waited to be called in for our interview. The movie was the 2008 hit classic *The Express: The Ernie Davis Story*. It's a true story based on Ernie Davis, a man born into poverty who overcame racism to become the first Black player to win the 1961 Heisman Trophy.

The employee said, "Overcoming adversity is essential to marketing success at our company. This movie is a great example of that. Please enjoy, and we'll come get each of you, one at a time momentarily."

I sat there and watched this movie for a few minutes. Ten minutes went by. Then twenty-five. At this point, people stopped talking to each other, put down their belongings, and watched the movie in silence. After a while, a few people just got up and left. I would envy them later, but at the time, I was committed to a career in sports marketing. I looked up the running time of the film on my phone: two hours and ten minutes.

After almost an hour, I was finally called in. I walked into this man's office who was sitting at a desk with no computer. His name was Brian. There was just a phone (clearly for show) and a stack of manila folders. The walls in his office were completely bare and pearly white. The only items in it were a desk, two chairs, and a bookshelf behind him. It looked like a room that posed as an office during the day but transformed into a low-budget porn set at night.

Brian started asking me questions that seemed surprising for a job with the White Sox.

1. Do you have reliable transportation?
2. How long can you run before getting tired?
3. Which type of animal would you be to survive in the wild?
4. How extroverted are you?

If I was being honest, I would have told him:

1. I borrowed my mom's car to get here.
2. About thirty feet.
3. A bird so I could avoid the wild.
4. I'm kind of an introvert.

After a series of BS answers, someone came in and whispered something into his ear, and he left with no explanation. After I briefly checked my phone to see what time it was, I noticed something odd about the bookshelf. As I looked closer, the books were all sealed together. They were fake. I shouldn't have been surprised because Brian didn't necessarily look like a person who read books but rather a person who would seal them shut in an effort not to read.

He came back in and said, "All right, let's go!"

He led me out of his office and back into the movie room where seven of the fifteen candidates remained. He turned off the movie which was right at the part where Ernie Davis is awarded the Heisman Trophy. They brought in a boom box (in 2009) and played *Jock Jams* (still good) for us to get pumped up for the day. We stood up in the half circle and clapped our hands together while each of us went around and said our own names. Then their sales reps grabbed each of us as we headed outside.

In the parking lot, our sales rep explained that each of us would be riding with them on their daily sales calls. Our job was to observe them see what makes them successful salespeople. We were instructed to take notes that we would present to Brian back at the office at the end of the day.

My sales rep for the day was Kyle. He was twenty-four years old and was wearing a wrinkled white dress shirt that was untucked. He greeted me with a high five and noted that he was taller than me. He opened his driver's side door and pulled a long black tie out from the side panel located at the bottom of the door. As he was putting on his tie in the parking lot, he told me that we would stop for breakfast before we started the day. While we were driving, I wanted to ask him questions because I was confused about this interview process.

"So what was with that movie?" I asked.

"I dunno, they always play weird shit," Kyle replied.

"How long have you been at this job?"

"It's my eleventh day."

"Cool… Where are we going?"

"Just observe. Ask questions later."

I felt like Ethan Hawke in *Training Day*, except I die. We drove for a while toward the city and started to head to the south side of Chicago.

Once we got down there, he parked and said, "Okay, we're here. Hop out."

He turned around to the back seat, grabbed a stack of White Sox tickets, and tossed them to me.

I asked, "Great, what do I do with these?"

"Sell them."

"To who?"

"I dunno, just go door-to-door. I'll pick you up right here at 5:00 p.m."

"It's 11:00 a.m."

"I think the record for a first timer is forty tickets sold. Good luck!"

"Are we still getting breakfast?"

He didn't respond and sped away in his gray car. I watched the car drive away for almost a minute, thinking he would eventually turn back around and say "Just kidding!" As I finally lost sight of the car in the distance, I sat down on the curb trying to remember my earlier excitement. I'm a baseball fan. Okay, sure, I'll sell some Sox tickets. I marched over to the first house I saw and knocked on the door. A woman opened her screened door to the best sales pitch of all time:

"White Sox tickets!" I said.

"What?" the woman asked.

(I visualized this job as a hotdog vendor at a baseball game.)

"Hello, my name is John. I'm selling White Sox tickets. Do you like baseball?"

"Uh, not really."

"Are you sure?"

"Yes."

"Okay, have a nice day!"

It was clear that not only was I a terrible salesman, but there was no way I was going door-to-door selling tickets all day. Seeing as I completed one sales call, I thought I'd treat myself to lunch. I walked ten minutes to a local Burger King where I would stay at for the entire day. I think I ate four Whoppers. I thought about calling my dad to pick me up but realized that would've been worse than what I was currently doing. Around 4:45 p.m., I walked back to the spot where Kyle left me for dead. He pulled up and rolled the window down.

"Hey! How'd you do?" he asked.

"Not great," I replied.

"How many did you sell?"

"None."

"None? You were out here all day!"

"I'm sorry. I don't think I'm cut out for this job."

"Dude, we're going to be in so much trouble."

"How many did you sell?"

"None because you had all of the tickets."

"So what did you do all day?"

"Just get in."

We drove back in complete silence—Kyle, because he was furious with me, and I, because I was thinking about all the terrible things I witnessed during my five-hour lunch at Burger King.

Millennials

*Why does everything have to be "us"? Is
there no "me" left? Why can't there be some
things just for me? Is that so selfish?*

I'M A MILLENNIAL, and like many others, I've had a
complicated relationship with work from the beginning. I entered the job market in 2009 right after the
economic collapse of 2008. I was constantly told that
things "were getting better" by older people and that
being miserable was simply a rite of passage for recent
graduates. We had to listen to people call us entitled,
selfish, and disloyal. We were told that if we went
to college and worked hard, we would find a good
job. Upon graduation, we were met with a massive
recession and employers taking advantage of recent
graduates, paying them nothing while expecting
everything. Instead of opening the door to a career,

a college degree now allowed you the opportunity to vie for extremely competitive unpaid internships. We were sold a falsehood.

Let's address entitlement. Millennials didn't invent participation trophies or sportsmanship awards. The feeling of being "special" was created by the environment we were raised in. Growing up, we were taught that we could be anything we wanted. Movies and TV shows were always about "Follow your dreams," "Money isn't the most important thing," and "Find something you love, and you'll never work a day in your life." Though they may have thought it, parents of millennials didn't tell us, "Listen, you can't be anything you want to be. Don't follow your dreams. Money is more important than doing something you love." Raising a child in this type of environment has some residual effects of entitlement, which I am guilty of.

Right after I graduated college, I sent out the TV-and-radio résumé tape I had created while working various internships during undergrad. I sent over eighty applications to local TV stations across the country from Tampa, Florida, to Fairbanks, Alaska. I got a phone interview from KOAM-TV–Pittsburgh for a weekend sports reporter position. Okay, great, this is how it's supposed to work. After all, I secured internships, worked hard, and did everything I was supposed to do to land this type of job.

I got on the phone with their station director, and he started asking me about my background and experience. I told him I would be thrilled for the opportunity to cover teams like the Steelers, Penguins, Pirates, and any other Pittsburgh sports references I could remember.

After my long-winded pitch about my love for Pittsburgh sports, there was a long pause on the other end of the phone.

Then he said, "Oh no. The station is in Pittsburg, Kansas."

I asked, "Where's that?"

"Kansas."

"I don't understand."

I was so confused because not only had I just learned (at twenty-two years old) that two different towns could have the same name, but I took this phone interview to work in Pittsburgh, not Pittsburg. He explained this position would be covering local high school sports for their town of 18,769 people. I decided to decline the opportunity not just because their $16,000-a-year salary couldn't support my crippling student loan debt but because I didn't want to work in a small market.

I thought it was completely normal to get a job in a large market after college because my résumé tape was good and I had a great experience at my internships. What I learned is that I was extremely naive to think that a person gets a broadcasting job in a major market right out of college. Your first job in TV broadcasting is almost always in an extremely small market, and then you work your way up to larger ones.

It didn't make any sense to me because millennials were told that, if we worked hard, we'd find a job immediately, be paid well, and get to "live our truth." But that didn't happen for most of us, and for the ones it did, we're happy for you and certainly don't secretly hate you.

I remember listening to a podcast in which they had a Harvard psychology professor talking to a large group of students. They wanted to know the secret to happiness. They started yelling and cheering, hoping for the answer everyone wants to hear. The professor said, "You all want to know what the secret to happiness is? Lower your expectations." It has been cited in several studies, most notably in a 2014 study from University College London. Specifically, they found that, for happiness to increase, it was not enough just for things to be going well; but things needed to be going better than expected, which led to the idea that lowering expectations could help facilitate happiness.

I think about that quote every day as I vacillate between narrowly pursuing my actual goals and being content with what I already have. I struggle with it because the professor is both right and wrong. He's right because, if we did lower our expectations, it would be easier to accomplish or exceed our goals. I wish I would've been enamored with the law or wanted to become a dentist. I wished I liked fixing things to become a contractor or an electrician. I'm not suggesting pursuing careers in these fields is by any means easy, just that there is a specific roadmap to certain professions.

Unfortunately for me, I love writing, acting, and sports entertainment. You can get an MFA, study at a conservatory, intern at radio stations, join improv groups, and write a book about your job failures; and it still doesn't work out. There are thousands of out-of-work chefs, actors, singers, writers, painters, musicians, broadcasters, and poets. If they are working, they are grateful to be doing so. I can assure you none of those people lowered their expectations because they are doing what they love. That is where science lacks nuance. If your singular definition of happiness is the pinnacle of your field, you are less likely to make it that far. Success is motivating. If you don't allow yourself to feel happiness as you progress, however small, discouragement will win out. Our parents were right for telling us we were special because, despite it being basically statistically impossible, it gave us hope and the confidence to try rather than being cynical. If people lowered their expectations for happiness, we wouldn't have some of the greatest inventions and art in the world. If Steve Jobs lowered his expectations, we'd all be using fucking Blackberries.

Millennials will never see the same amount of wealth as their parents. They have suffered two unprecedented economic recessions. They have been forced to work longer for less money. Millennials have to wait longer to buy a home, have children, get married, and (insert any other big life event). We have more debt than assets. We are described as having no loyalty to companies but only because companies never showed us any. The 12.5 percent unemployment rate of millennials is higher than Gen X and baby boomers. We are deferring our student loans because we are broke. People describe millennials as lazy, aloof, and entitled. What you'll actually find is they're resourceful, hardworking, and empathetic. They will make far-better managers, VPs, and

CEOs than the previous generations. They'll create a workplace for the future that will benefit everyone. They'll put an emphasis on employees taking mental-health days. They'll encourage taking vacations and not scrutinize over PTO hours. They'll trust their employees to work from home and not freak out about not being in the office. They'll relinquish their power for the betterment of their culture, society, and the environment. Millennials have seen and experienced the negative outcomes of power and greed. Most importantly, they know what not to do.

Watching TV
with Subtitles

*My name is George, I'm unemployed,
and I live with my parents.*

YOU MIGHT BE in a situation where you find yourself moving back home with your parents, and regardless of what age you are, it's not ideal. The first thing you need to do is shed the shame. There is an unprecedented recession going on. Nobody is going to fault you for moving home, and if they do, they're heartless assholes. Shame will only hinder your growth and turn you into a nightmare for your parents who don't need the added stress because, ya know, they're old. You're not a failure for moving back home, and your parents don't think you're a failure either. They understand your situation and, frankly, are very nice to let you come home to eat their food, watch their premier cable channels, and mooch off their spotty Wi-Fi. Shed the shame early because, if you don't, it will be hard to present your best self to prospective hiring managers; and they will notice it, especially when your parents barge in while you're on your Zoom interview.

I know it's difficult to be nice to your parents because they have a unique ability to drive you crazy. Remember, they are just human beings who are trying to do their best, kind of like you. They thought you would never return home again, so this isn't ideal for them either unless you have parents who are sweethearts and were overjoyed when you came home. This was not my experience. I came home twice—once after I graduated college and once during a time in which I had a total of ten jobs in two years or as I refer to it as the "dark times." Again, we'll get to that later.

My parents immediately turned my bedroom into a guest room a week after I left for college. I'm one of five kids, so vacant real estate was snatched up quickly in my house. My parents were not thrilled when I came back home the first time. I'm not sure if they remember the second time because having five kids erases about 65 percent of your memory.

Here are a few things you need to remember if you want things to be peaceful during your short (hopefully) time there. Here are dos and don'ts:

Dos

- Have "something to do" today.
- Create a list of all their usernames and passwords and print it out on physical pieces of paper next to all relevant devices.
- Clean.
- Explain the cloud.
- Listen about all their physical ailments.
- See your grandparents.

Don'ts

- Bring up old childhood gripes.
- Talk politics.
- Discuss youth sport experiences.
- Talk about your relationships.
- Talk about your job hunt.
- Talk.

You might not be great with technology, but to your parents, you're Steve Jobs. I know they're hopeless and will forget everything you told them the second after you leave, but try to be nice to them while you're home. Technology is nothing without the correct username and password, something every parent forgets. My mother could not find her password at gunpoint. Be patient and try to resolve any tech query online before your parents force you to call a semiconscious customer service rep on the telephone. My dad still cannot understand how Uber works. I've explained it to him a hundred times, and I've used it with him while in the car. Things that still puzzle him: (1) How do they find you? (2) How do they know your name? and (3) How did we get out of the car without paying?

Maybe the most important advice I can give you is to learn how to watch TV with subtitles. Don't give your parents a hard time about it because, remember, you could be living out on the street! Be sympathetic to your parent's rapid hearing loss and say, "I love reading while I'm watching TV!"

However out of touch and sleepy your parents seem, you haven't scratched the surface until you're living there again. When you're watching *Cast Away* with your parents and they fall asleep before Tom Hanks gets on the island, resist the rage and remember you will eventually turn into some version of that someday. As one ages, you start to begrudgingly accept subtitles. If you're watching a British drama with quick, pithy dialogue, maybe some dictation might be nice. Just something to think about.

Start seeing your parents as regular people, not just your parents. Get to know them again as an adult. Find out how their friends are doing. Be patient when they launch into an epic saga when you ask them for directions. It gives them great pleasure. They feel it's the only wisdom they have left to give the younger generation. Do not be a jerk and ruin that for them. Suppress your retort of "Just give me the address." Be patient when your parents can't remember the names of any actor, movie title, or their own children's name. They're happy you're there, and remember, it's (probably) only temporary.

The goal of a parent who has five kids consists of one main concept: just keep them alive.

Their responsibilities for their children are primitive: feed them, put a roof over their heads, and educate them. Dreams and happiness are luxuries. There's just no time for it. To prove this, I would ask my parents, "What's more important? A happy child or a self-sufficient child?" Their answer was always the latter.

My mom wasn't surprised by my choice to pursue a career in comedy. She said that a parent can tell the personality of their children early on. My family has a vault of VHS home videos that were taped by my dad throughout our childhood. My mom showed me a tape she said perfectly exhibited her children's personalities at a young age.

It was 1989, and I was playing with my two older sisters Theresa and Anna in the backyard. Theresa was six years old, Anna was five, and I was three. The sky was getting dark because there was a storm coming. My mom shouted for all of us to quickly pick up our toys, put them in our toy bin, and head into the house. Theresa, who is a free spirit and has a certain disregard for the rules, didn't listen and kept playing with her toys while she danced around the house. Anna, who is a little anxious and very much a rule follower, did exactly what she was told. She frantically ran all over the yard picking up toys and putting them into the bin, deathly afraid of the storm. I was a good listener but not a rule follower. I started taking out the toys that Anna had put in the bin and placed them back into the yard. I got in trouble, but it was funny. Therefore, totally worth it.

Creative pursuits were encouraged by my parents but only to a point. Once the creative pursuit became too powerful, it was to be killed immediately and ideally, never talked about again. While I was living at home, I would still drive to the city to do comedy while applying for jobs. I refrained from talking about it around my parents because my mom would repeatedly say, "We get it, John. You like comedy." She didn't really want to hear about it unless it would produce a job to get me out of the house.

When I first started doing comedy, my parents were mildly amused. That sentiment faded with each passing day I wasn't "discovered." At the time I was living home, I had been performing improv and writing sketch comedy for almost five years, which, to my parents, was four and a half years too many because I wasn't on *Saturday Night Live* yet. One night, all of us were watching TV when, all of a sudden, my mom's interest was piqued.

"How can we watch your comedy?" she asked.

"I've been asking you and Dad to come to come to a show for the past five years," I said.

"They're so far away."

"They're all in the city, an hour from your house. My friend's parents just flew in from Houston to see her perform."

"Maybe we'll come to one soon."

"I have one next Friday."

"Can you please take the pizza out of the oven? I think the timer is about to go off."

Because I knew they would never come to see one live, which is by far the best way to experience a comedy show, I had an idea. Recently, my improv group had performed in an improv festival where our twenty-five-minute set was taped and put on Vimeo to watch. It was probably the best show we'd ever done where we received huge laughs from the crowd. I told my parents we could all watch it right now. They were on board probably because they were "officially" fulfilling the burden of watching their son pursue his passion. We got up from the couch, grabbed pizza, and then sat back down. My parents were sitting next to each other on our family room couch while I was off to the right in our recliner chair where I had a good vantage point of my parents' reaction. After minutes of troubleshooting because of poor Wi-Fi, the show started playing, but I wasn't watching. I was transfixed on my parent's faces, hoping they would enjoy it. My dad's face resembled the puzzled look my dog gives me when I attempt to speak to him. Throughout the entire twenty-five-minute show, at no point did they laugh. At no point did they move. The show ended with a large applause by the audience as the video stopped.

"So what did you think?" I asked.

"Wow, that was long!" my mom replied.

"What about you, Dad?"

"That sure was a lot of ad-libbing. Well, good night!" Dad said.

After my dad headed upstairs to bed, I sat there confused. Did he not understand what improv is? Does he go to the pool and say, "Wow, that's a lot of water!" I asked my mom if she liked it.

She said, "Oh yes, it was very funny."

This meant nothing to me because my mom will say anything to get herself out of a conversation she's not interested in having. She quickly switched the channel to HGTV to watch *House Hunters International* with the sound off.

The Art of Killing Time

Just remember, it's not a lie…if you believe it.

IN DECEMBER OF 2009, I headed to Downtown Chicago for what was my most promising job interview since I graduated college—an entry-level telephone sales rep. It was with an advertising company that primarily sold *Yellow Page* ads in physical-paper telephone directories during the time of the iPhone, Google, and a major recession. At this point, I had been unemployed for about six months following graduation. Sequestered in my parent's basement working on beating Grand Theft Auto 3 for the fourth time, I desperately needed a salaried position.

I got off on the sixty-eighth floor and headed toward the front desk. I was greeted by a nice old woman named Rhea. She had short white hair and black glasses. She said I would be interviewing with

Eric who was in charge of recruiting. He was running late, so she told me to relax and take a seat while I waited.

"Take a few pieces of candy while you wait. He'll probably be about fifteen to twenty minutes."

I got up and went over to the most confusing candy bowl I had ever seen. It consisted of several mini candy bars surrounded by loose mints. I figured that, if I had to wait twenty minutes, I could quickly eat a few pieces.

Eric busted through the door and headed directly toward me. He reached out to shake my hand (which used to be a thing people did). I reluctantly extended my hand with dried chocolate smears while likely giving off a constipated smile. Eric was short and bald with thick black glasses, closely resembling the musical artist Moby. He asked me several business questions about my work ethic. Many of these questions are very typical in sales interviews. I was feeding him answers about going above and beyond and how I always wanted to be number one in everything I did. Mixing in sports analogies with guys during sales interviews is always a plus.

The interview was going very well. I was giving Eric exactly what he wanted to hear, and then we came to his final question.

"John, has there ever been a time when you were in a leadership position and things didn't go according to plan? If so, how did you adapt to it?"

I drew a blank. I couldn't think of anything. I started looking up at the ceiling—a clear indication the person doesn't have an answer. Then I remembered an incident when I was an RA in college during undergrad. In my two years as an RA, we had one real fire. It was my responsibility, once the alarm went off, to knock on everyone's door, which consisted of about twenty-five to thirty guys, and get them out of the building. It was the most basic evacuation procedure known to man. During the one real fire evacuation I was involved in, the fire was started from a burnt Pop-Tart in a resident's toaster oven. The smoke set off the alarm. It was not the least bit dangerous. The student who started the fire put it out himself in five seconds with a cup of water. Because of the smoke, the alarm went off; however, we had to evacuate everyone. I knocked on every resident's door and led them out down the stairs. It took about four minutes to evacuate everybody. It was an extremely routine and uneventful process.

When people give advice on how to ace your interview, they always end with "Just be yourself," like it's that simple. For several months, I had been myself in previous interviews, but I had gotten nowhere. I couldn't blame them because even I was beginning to hate myself. I was desperate and wanted to end the interview on a high note.

"I would say a time I was in a leadership position and things didn't go according to plan was when I saved my residents from a burning building when I was an RA in college."

"Oh my god," he replied. He started to lean in from his desk.

"Yes, it was a pretty traumatic ordeal. During my time as resident assistant, we had a fire in our building. As an RA, I devised a very specific fire evacuation plan which involved me going up and down the hall notifying all the residents on my floor to make sure that everyone was out of their room. I think I had around fifty to seventy-five guys living on my floor at the time. After I got everyone out of their rooms, the plan was to take them down the south stairwell and outside to safety. Well, as I quickly found out, that wasn't going to be an option. The fire was started by a student who was smoking a cigarette in his room and dropped it in the trash. He did not live on my floor. I was the RA on duty that particular night, so I responded upstairs. I got everyone out of their rooms and safely brought them down to the hallway corridor where they were waiting for my instruction. Now, our protocol is to evacuate everyone out through the south stairwell. The entire south stairwell was on fire. We couldn't get out that way. So I had to think of a way to get these guys out safely. Just then, I remembered we had a storage room that was located down in the basement that led outside through a side door. It was the safest way to get the guys out of the building. We often overlooked the storage space in the basement because it was always locked. Luckily, all the RA keys had access to the lockbox which had the storage key in it. I ran over to the RA room, got the key, and unlocked the storage room where I led all of our residents out of the building to safety. We almost lost one of my residents in the smoke; so I went back, found him, and carried him out. Just some light smoke inhalation, nothing serious. The building could have gone up in flames, but when you're a leader, failure is not an option. So that would be a time when I was in a leadership position and adapted when things didn't go according to plan."

I was getting emotional by the end of the story. The thought of all that would be very traumatic. I still have no idea where all that came from; but they bought it because, two days later, I got the job. I went home later that afternoon, ripped off my tie, took off my dress shirt, and hung up my jacket. As I emptied my pockets, I rediscovered several wrappers—three Twixes, two Snickers, two Milk Ways, two Heath bars, and one Baby Ruth.

On my first day at my new job, they unveiled our new up-and-coming "digital products" which consisted of social media and creating websites. This was a big deal back in 2010. Upper management was ecstatic about what they called "the digital advantage" which focused on being prevalent in both print and, now, digital media.

Our elderly bosses were amazed but also heavily threatened by digital marketing, social media, and, most of all, the internet. They would desperately try to prove the benefit of the print *Yellow Pages* to their junior staff every day, similar to how parents try to persuade their children that vegetables taste good.

"Let me explain something to you, John, that you might not be aware of since you're new to the business. More people are using the Internet, not just for reports but for everything! Our clients still look in the *Yellow Page* book, but now they can find the same information online even faster!"

After all, you see, our company was entering the "Viral World." How did I know this? It was mandatory for every employee to have a six-inch laminated card taped to the top of our computer monitor which stated in big bold letters "WE NOW LIVE IN A VIRAL WORLD."

My official title was telephone account representative or TAR, which was apropos because we were lower than low in the corporate hierarchy. The tier of sales people ranked from top to bottom were regional account manager (RAM), account manager (AM), account representative (AR), telephone account executive (TAE), and TAR or, as you might refer to them, telemarketers. Not that we could. Saying the word *telemarketer* was like saying Voldemort. It was strictly forbidden. We were instructed to identify ourselves to clients as "marketing consultants."

My boss told us, "Telemarketers are people who sell useless crap over the phone to random strangers and only care about one thing, which is closing the deal."

I had difficulty seeing the distinction because that was the very definition of my job. My primary function was to sit in a six- to eight-foot cube for eight hours a day and make phone calls to local business owners around the Chicago land area and try to get them to spend at least $9.50 to $1,000 per month on advertising. Over the phone. In the *Yellow Pages*.

During a recession. They wanted a high volume of calls, talk time, and, most importantly, sales. We had mandatory duties each day that required us to make at least one hundred calls and have three to four hours of talk time on the phone. They called these KPIs which stands for "key performance indicators." Every TAR's phone was hooked up to a recording device so the manager could listen in on our calls. It also kept track of the number of calls you made per day along with your hours of talk time, so you couldn't fudge your productivity. At the end of each day, all TARs would meet to report their number of calls and talk time for the day.

Any telemarketer knows that there are two types of calls. Calls and real calls. Real calls are dials to business owners with the intent to persuade them into buying something. Calls are dials to anyone that is not a prospective customer or client with absolutely zero intention of selling anything or speaking to a real live human being. You would say things at this job that you thought would never come out of your mouth: "Mr. Customer, I definitely think a semibold listing in the Cook County directory will without a doubt help grow your colonic irrigation business."

It is impossible to make one hundred real calls in one day. It's also impossible to make fifty real calls in one day. During a typical eight-hour workday, I would often choose to just make calls, which would mostly go to disconnected numbers. We would get new spreadsheets each day that would consist of hundreds and hundreds of numbers for us to call. For me, finding a disconnected number was more exciting than making a sale. I would carefully put each one into my own private list of disconnected numbers accumulated over the year. When you have a quota of making one hundred calls a day to people who vehemently hate you, you need a break, so you sprinkle in a few disconnected numbers during each day to keep your sanity. To increase talk time, I would call people like my mom, friends, and, quite often, my own cell phone. One day, I logged 110 calls with seven minutes of talk time. My family and friends were busy that day, probably working. I could tell how bad my day went by the number of fake voicemails I left on my own phone.

Beep! "Hey, Mike, this is John from the Yellow Pages. I just wanted to give ya a shout. Hadn't heard from ya in a while. I wanted to check up and see if you were still interested in that print ad we talked about. I emailed you a copy of the ad, so just shoot me back an email when you get it. Talk to you later. Go Bears! Ha ha. All right, take care."

Beep! "Hey, Rich, John here givin' you a call again. Boy, you're a tougher guy to get a hold of than the president. We got that website all set up for you. We just need you to sign that contract I faxed over this morning. Remember, you got to spend money to make money. Say hi to Karen for me."

Beep! "Hey, B-rad, it's ya boy, Johnny. Sorry I missed your call. I was in Costa Rica on a company trip. All the top sales reps were out last week. I'm feelin' a little under weather today if ya know what I'm saying. Ugh. I don't have to tell you what that's about, you son of a bitch. Ha ha! Give me a buzz."

To say I hated this job would be an understatement. When you hate a job this much, you fantasize about something bad happening that will prevent you from having to go into work. For me, I would often think about a cab hitting me while walking on my way to work. Nothing serious. Maybe just running over my foot so I couldn't walk the rest of the way. Possibly get some crutches. Sometimes, while I was waiting for the train in the morning, I would look over the edge saying to myself, "If I just stick my elbow out slightly, I might get a bone bruise and have to go the hospital. Either way, I won't have to step foot in that office today." Sometimes people say they hate their job, but until you are willing to inflict pain on yourself not to go, it's just an inconvenience.

I'm not sure who had more disdain for one another, me or the unfortunate people I was call-ing. The prospective customers we were dialing were small- to medium-sized business owners who had lost everything in the recession. Our business model was, seeing as they lost so much already, maybe they were willing to lose a little bit more. I can't tell you how many times my life was threatened on these calls by customers. Easily over fifty times. One of the benefits of checking your soul at the door is that you become bulletproof. Nothing a customer said to me could hurt my feelings because, at that point, I didn't have any. I once had a customer tell me that he would buy something from me if I could prove I had a college degree. I was in such desperate need for a sale (as I would always on a performance plan) that I called up my alma mater to ask if they could send me a copy of my transcript.

As a telemarketer, you get access to each com-pany's do-not-call list which, as you can imagine, is never ending. Sometimes, however, for the sake of morale, you make an exception. We could see how many times a customer had requested to be taken off the do-not-call list. We had a former customer who used to advertise with us years ago. He had a painting business, but it went under because our company "stole money from him" by not generating any new clientele through our advertising. Fair point. However, the blame is at least fifty-fifty for believing us. Additionally, he was rude, racist, and crude to our reps. He had requested to be taken off our list eighteen different times and would still leave us threatening voicemails. I tried to forget about this job the second I left the building, but this particular customer stuck with me. Because I was contributing zero in sales, I felt it was my duty to keep morale high. So late on a Friday afternoon around 4:50 p.m., I decided to give him a call on speaker in a conference room, which was not on a recorded line. He threatened to shoot us in the streets, assassinate the sitting US president, and take down the entire company. Right on brand as I suspected. We all died laughing on the floor which, in a weird way, brought our team closer together. This position was not anyone's desired career, and we were all fully aware of the ridiculousness of our jobs. It made working with each other more enjoyable and made our work experience more tolerable—for a least a few minutes.

Remember to Laugh

These stories have not been embellished, because they need no embellishment. They are simply, horrifyingly, the story of my life as a short, stocky, slow-witted bald man.

AS MY TIME went on at this job, I started caring less and less. It got to a point where, when I would leave for lunch, I would just leave my phone of the hook to acquire talk time but mostly so I didn't have to talk to anyone. After the first two months of training were over and I was alone at my desk unsupervised, I applied for other jobs the entire time. For a good eight months, the company was paying me to look for other jobs. I tallied up all my sales (didn't take long) and calculated that I made significantly more money from the company than they made from me during my year and a half working there. I didn't think things could get any worse, but then I accidently smashed my face into my boss's new car.

I and two colleagues were coming back from lunch in my coworker Jenni's car. It was a Friday in July, so everyone was in a good mood. We just entered the parking lot and pulled into the only vacant spot which was right next to our boss's new car. Dawn had mentioned her new black Lexus several times that morning, so we knew it was hers. My two colleagues, Jenni and Amanda, were sitting in the front seat; and I was in the right back seat. We parked and started to get out of the car. In Jenni's car, the front seat would fold down; and the person getting out of the back seat would have to climb over the folded-down front seat, maneuver around the front seat belt, and hop out. I've always had issues about getting out of cars. I'm about five feet, ten inches; but I have clown feet (size 13), which makes it difficult to get out of small cars, Ubers, taxis, and all back seats of cars. As I lifted my right leg to exit the car, my right foot got caught on the seat belt strap. I came barreling out of the car as my right knee slammed on the ground. As I was falling forward, my left foot got caught in the seat belt strap as my left knee slammed down into the hot asphalt. There was no stopping my body as it was catapulted directly into the driver's side door of my boss's new car. *Bam*! My head rocketed so hard into her car there was a permanent indentation of my face in her door. I had never suffered a concussion or whiplash, so experiencing both at the same time was a bit much. At this point, my whole body is out of the car except for my feet which are still stuck in the back seat of Jenni's car.

I blacked out for a few seconds; and as I came to, Jenni and Amanda were crying so hard from laughter that I thought they too were going to pass out. I plead with them to help me because now people were starting to stare out of the window. I was kneeling, concussed, and bleeding with my feet stuck in a car. With my nose bleeding, the girls helped me untangle my feet from the seat belt and walked me back into the office. I went to the restroom to clean myself up. My dress pants were ripped at the knees and covered with blood. I went back to my desk and tried to forget about the pain by applying for other jobs.

Then Amanda came over to my desk and asked, "When are you going to tell Dawn?"

I had completely forgotten about that part.

"Maybe she won't notice," I said.

"You have to tell her," Amanda replied.

I had three different bosses during my time at this company, and I'm sure they all couldn't wait to not see my face anymore the second after they left work. Now it was indented in one of their car doors.

I applied for a few more jobs and then headed to Dawn's office. As I entered, she gave me a look that can only be described as "Are you lost?" I hadn't made a sale in months, and I think she forgot I still worked there. I asked her if I could talk to her; and she started to smile a little because, in her mind, maybe I was turning a corner by asking her advice on how to become a salesperson. On the contrary, I wanted to tell her that I smashed my face into her new car. I explained the entire story of what happened to her; and of course, she did not believe it because, I mean, how could you? If someone told me that story, I wouldn't believe it.

I begrudgingly said, "Come with me. I'll show you."

We went outside, and I showed her the dent my face had made. It was sort of cool looking because it reminded me of Han Solo in carbonite. She was very angry and in disbelief that her brand-new car had my face in it. She also knew that I had no money to pay for this because I was just out of college and broke and had only made three sales in seven months. That was the last time I talked to Dawn during my time there. She had insurance and eventually fixed her car.

I was probably the most forgettable salesperson that ever worked for her, but I'll bet she never forgot my face.

Things were looking bleak as I was hanging on by a thread at this point. I had trouble summoning the energy to carry on, but then something great happened. Maybe the best thing ever. Our jobs got liquidated. That's right. I know it's hard to believe that, in the age of the iPhone and Google, the work-force wouldn't need a print Yellow Page telephone sales rep. Now, I always knew this would eventually happen, but I expected/prayed it would've happened much sooner. When our boss broke the news to all the TARs in the conference room, literal tears streamed down my face. I had so suppressed my feelings for over a year that I had forgotten what happiness was. It was like being rescued off a desert island. They explained that we would be getting severance packages on our way out. Even more tears. I wasn't the only TAR crying, but mine were for very different reasons. We all sat silent for a couple of minutes.

My boss, who genuinely felt bad, said, "How's everyone holding up?"

During the year and a half I was at this company, I think I spoke to management a total of three times, almost always non-work related. I wanted to be seen, not heard. I knew I was never going to be good at this job, so I just tried to be pleasant and quiet. But because I hadn't felt such jubilation in the past year, I wiped the tears from my face, tried to suppress a huge smile, and said, "Well, as good as you can be at a time like this."

If you're at a place you're not happy with, whether it's a job or at home with your parents, try to find things to laugh at. They are the life blood that will carry you through the dark times. They did for me. You have to ride the wave of chaos because, if you don't, you'll drown. As much disdain as I had for this job, the people I worked with were very nice. They made an effort to support me, but there was nothing they could've done that was going to make me a successful salesperson. That was my responsibility. It's not that I wasn't capable of doing it, but I didn't care. I didn't believe in the product we were selling, and I didn't like pressuring people into buying something I knew had no value. Many of us have worked at companies where their products and services are bullshit. A way to get through it is to compartmentalize the situation. Surround yourself with things that make you remember who you are, what you care about, and where you ultimately want to be because you know it's not here. I do believe you learn something at every job, some things more pleasant than others. What I learned from this job was survival skills, which I would desperately need later in my career. I never believed I could've worked at a place I hated for more than two weeks. But I was able to stick it out for a year and a half. Find the little successes wherever you can. To me, that was a huge victory.

The Dark Times

I don't want hope. Hope is killing me. My dream is to become hopeless. When you're hopeless, you don't care.

From March of 2013 to March of 2015, I had ten different jobs. I was broke and desperately trying to make ends meet so I could still live in the city of Chicago and not have to move back with my parents (see chapter 6). I was a marketing specialist, paid marketing intern, barista, IT rep, office manager, copywriter, copywriter again, customer service rep, advertising account coordinator, and, finally, social media coordinator.

This was the most difficult time of my life. I was in a difficult position because I had just received my graduate degree, but I didn't have a lot of experience. That is a bad formula for someone trying to secure a job during a recession. Employers for entry-level jobs assumed I was out of their salary range because of my graduate degree, and employers for the mid-level jobs passed because of my lack of experience. The jobs I had during this time were all freelance, contract, or internship-type roles at start-ups. Again, not a great formula during a recession. I applied to hundreds of other jobs at bigger, more established companies but never heard back from them. I didn't have any control over my life and felt helpless.

Luckily, my time working as a Yellow Pages sales rep gave me survival skills and the empathy of a sociopath. I couldn't believe what my life had become. I had so many dreams and wasn't living any of them. In fact, I was aggressively heading in the opposite direction. To get through this time, I did two things. I laughed/cried my way through it and went into survival mode. Survival mode happens during a bad time in your life where you have to resort to Machiavellian tactics to survive it. You're solely looking out for yourself because your life is in shambles, and you'll do anything to escape it by any means necessary. Unfortunately, this means that some people or companies may get burned in the process. It's not personal; it's survival.

I worked as a marketing specialist for a start-up company that specialized in MacBook repairs for liquid spills. You could say I had a knack for legit, reliable jobs. Minutes after offering me the job, I accepted it and closed on an apartment in the city. Two months later, I was let go because they "couldn't pay me anymore" because my minimum $8.25 an hour salary accounted for 70 percent of their cash flow. This would be a recurring theme.

This position reported directly to the CEO because there weren't any other people between us. The company consisted of eight people, five of which repaired MacBooks and one customer service rep. The office was a tiny suite in a large office building in Downtown Chicago that could only fit two people at a time. I wrote blogs and created other marketing content for them.

After a month working there, my boss set a meeting with me to go over a brilliant marketing campaign he thought of the night before.

He walked in with a massive white sign with our company's name on it and said, "I want you to walk up and down Michigan Avenue holding up this sign."

Being the team player that I was, I said okay because, in my experience, this was a better marketing strategy than advertising in the *Yellow Pages*. On a hot summer day, I walked up and down the streets of Downtown Chicago holding a massive cardboard sign over my head, hoping people would be able to retain our website name, phone number, email address, and fax number as they drove forty miles per hour past me. A thought kept running through my head throughout the day as I was sweating through my now-see-through white company shirt with our liquid-stain logo on it: *This can't be my life.*

I felt like one of those wacky inflatable tubes they use at gas stations to catch people's attention, but unfortunately for me, I was alive and not having any fun. Growing up in the Chicagoland area, statistically, someone I knew must have seen me but has been nice enough to never to bring it up. I was a human billboard roaming around town, promoting a ridiculous service (see AppleCare). I had prepared to be mocked, and it would've been completely justified. Instead, I was pitied. Strangers on the street felt bad for me, which is unheard of on the streets of Chicago. If you encounter a stranger who is fire, protocol is to politely walk around them and ignore their screams of pain. A woman came up to me on the street and gave me two dollars, smiled, and walked away. She clearly thought I was homeless and that I was using this fake company for money. Our company logo of a stain probably didn't help. I politely accepted the two dollars as it turned out to be my bonus for the year.

Because of the year lease I had just signed on my apartment, I had to find another job quickly to pay rent. I applied for a paid internship with a security company that specialized in online background checks for employers. Already, it did not instill faith in their product because they hired me. Traditionally, you want to take a step forward in your career, not backward. I was fully aware that my life was headed in the wrong direction, but I couldn't stop it. The frustrating part was I tried to find legit jobs, but I couldn't land one. That leaves a twenty-six-year-old working as a paid marketing intern. My job titles were regressing—consultant → specialist → intern. Pretty soon, I was just going to be marketing human, which is me, unemployed, alone in my apartment.

This role had me doing some PR along with creating marketing materials. I would call various publications and ask them to do a story about our background check service. Management would instruct me to instill doubt in people's vetting systems. It didn't always work.

"How well do you really know the people you work with?" I asked.

"Actually, pretty well. They're all very nice," one publicist replied.

"Okay, thanks for your time!"

I was not great at sales.

My big marketing project during the three months I was there was creating a game for people to play at this cybersecurity expo we were attending. The event consisted of several start-ups who had their own booth, and customers would shop around to see if a software program would be a good fit for their company.

I spent an entire month writing and creating a fun interactive game to engage prospective customers. The objective was to attract people to our booth and scan their wristband, which had their contact information on it so we could follow up with them to sell our service. The game acted as a lead generation tactic. It was focused around all the funny and weird situations a company could find themselves in if they did not have our background check service. I modeled it off the board game Life. I created a mat on the floor where people would roll a dice, collect cards, and move along different squares on the mat as their fate was decided. I pitched it to our executive team two days before the expo, and they loved it. They thought it was really inventive and fun. For the first time in months, I felt like my work was appreciated and maybe I wasn't such a loser.

The day of expo came, and I was excited! I got there early to set up my game. I even did some last-minute rewrites the night before on a few cards. A few more employees came over to our booth and started setting up. As we got closer to opening, I was surprised I hadn't yet seen our boss. Right before they were about the open the doors to let everyone onto the floor, my boss came around the corner along with a strange man wearing raggedy cargo pants carrying a monkey.

My boss said, "Hey, John, we decided to do something a little different. We're going to hold off on your game and see how the monkey does. Bob is an animal trainer, and this is his monkey, Lou. We were going to set up on your mat where there's more room and see if the monkey can attract people to come over to the booth. The tag line is "Don't monkey around with people you don't know.""

I was shocked. I had worked on this stupid project for an entire month and had actually convinced myself that it was fun. I was so fucking mad but also happy because now I had a front-row seat to watch this idea crash and burn. I wrote five different drafts of my game, constructed a life-size mat that resembled a game board, and practiced hosting it several times at work. Now he thinks a monkey could do a better job than me? Fuck him and his stupid monkey.

I said, "Okay, if that's what you want."

Bear in mind, I was just an intern, so I had zero leverage in any situation. But I was praying it would fail and the monkey would be kidnapped, never to be seen again.

Bob, a seasoned carny who was friendly but also tremendously creepy, asked me to move off my mat. I tried to keep my distance because he smelled of feces and I hated him.

The doors opened as thousands of people filed in. I sat down and sipped my coffee, making no effort to do anything at this point.

In the distance, I heard a few people scream, "Oh my god, it's a little monkey!"

This was a cybersecurity conference, so it was as boring as it sounds. But when people saw a monkey in this mundane setting, they lost their minds. They rushed over to our booth to get their picture taken with Lou.

My boss said, "If you want a picture with Lou, you have to get wristband scanned by us."

People didn't hesitate. They happily held out their wrists to snap a picture with a monkey and his creepy trainer. More people started to come over to see the monkey. Lines started to form. At one point, there was a line of over a hundred people that went all the way back to the door.

Lou generated over five hundred new leads and, I assume, an incredible amount of revenue for the company. It was by far the biggest and most popular attraction at the expo. People were talking about it all over the floor, sharing pictures on social media using #DontMonkeyAround.

This honestly taught me a valuable lesson in marketing. Don't overthink it. Also beware that, when someone says a job is so easy a monkey could do it, sometimes they can.

Survival mode

Throughout my twenties, I drove with an empty popcorn bag in the glove compartment of my car. I was constantly broke and trying save money any way I could. This was my initiation to survival mode. Survival mode occurs when things are going so poorly you will do anything to regain any semblance of a normal life. One of the few things that made me happy during the dark times was going to the movie theater. I usually went by myself or with my improv friend Colin. Sometimes going to the movies by yourself is more enjoyable because you're not worrying if the other person is enjoying the film, especially if you're the one who recommended it. My wife thinks that people who go to the movies by themselves look "pathetic," which I'm totally fine with. Most people prefer to go at night, but I love a good 11:15 a.m. matinee with only two other people scarcely plotted in an empty theater. What's pathetic about that! What I couldn't do at the time was pay for popcorn. Movie theater concessions are a scam. The prices for movie theater popcorn, which is undoubtedly the best type of popcorn, have steadily risen since my teens. Trust me. I would always see at least one movie a week in the theater, and if you're getting popcorn every time, that adds up! People who run movie theaters should be grateful people are even showing up because of modern technology. That's why the ambiance of movie theaters has started to resemble Restoration Hardware because they figured out people can watch all of these movies at home for a much cheaper price. Also, most people under the age of forty know how easy it is to stream or torrent any movie for free off the internet.

To combat the cinema's capitalistic scheme, I would grab my empty popcorn bag from the glove compartment of my car, fold it, and then stuff it behind my back into the top of my pants. When I would enter the movie theater, I'd pay for my ticket (I'm not a monster) and then head into the bathroom or any type of arcade game area. I would discreetly remove the bag from behind my shirt and, with a single snap, pop it open, ready to be refilled for free. I had this down to a science when I was by myself, but when I took women on dates, it became much more complicated.

I first started implementing this strategy while living at home with parents. I had a date that I was getting ready for and was a little nervous about it. My mom came over and offered her usual words of wisdom, "Honey, just be yourself…well, not too much like yourself." Too little, too late, Mom. The popcorn bag was already in my pants.

When going on a date, I always had the popcorn bag tucked in the top of my pants before I picked them up or met them at the theater. After I paid for our tickets, I would always say, "Why don't you go to our seats, and I'll get popcorn for us." This way, I'd be left alone to do my thing. A couple important aspects about the popcorn bag that should be noted.

I would never have it completely empty. To provide credibility, I always leave a few extra kernels at the bottom of the bag. Sometimes I would make a slight tear in the top of the bag or fold it an extra time. To sell it, I needed the bag to look like it had recently been used but not used too much that it looked like it was snatched from the garbage. There was really an art of routinely making a popcorn bag look like it had recently been used over the course of an entire year. I probably bought one or maybe two popcorn bags each year, but only if they put a different design on the bag for some stupid superhero movie they were trying to promote. Otherwise, it was a surefire process.

When I was twenty-six, I took a date to the movies. Everything was going smoothly until she said something that almost crippled my entire operation.

"Why don't you grab our seats, and I'll get popcorn for us," I said.

"Actually, I'll just come with you because I'm not sure what I want," my date said.

"No!"

"What?"

"Is there something specific you'd like?"

"Well, I'm not sure if I want candy or popcorn."

"The popcorn here is really good."

"Can we just check it out?"

We eventually went together to the concession area where she ultimately decided she did want popcorn, and I had to pay $14 for something we could've easily had for free. Then I had to watch a two-and-a-half-hour movie with a slightly empty bag of popcorn in my pants. I moved gingerly when I got up and down from my seat so the bag wouldn't make a rustling sound. I watched the whole movie stiff as a board, barely blinking from the fear that she would hear the bag. Like many of my endeavors in my twenties, this relationship did not work out.

When I turned twenty-eight and finally had a decent enough salary to pay my bills, I stopped the popcorn operation. To all of my dates (four) I ever took to the movies from ages twenty-two to twenty-eight, the popcorn you ate with me was on the house. You're welcome. And briefly in my pants. I'm sorry.

After my three-month internship ended, I needed to find another job to keep me afloat. None of these jobs paid very well, so I couldn't afford long gaps of unemployment. I applied to hundreds of marketing jobs but with no response. I started walking around the neighborhood applying for bartending jobs (second time's a charm) and waiter jobs—

basically anything. I got a job as a barista at a local coffee shop. This allowed me to save money on food as I ate breakfast, lunch, and dinner there every single day. It also allowed me to gain twenty pounds in pastry weight. Even if I wasn't working, I would show up, head to the back room to see what food they were going to throw out that night, eat it, and leave. I would also take toilet paper from their bathroom back to my tiny studio apartment. After three months, which seemed to be my typical tenure at this point, I got a job working in the IT department for the Kellogg School of Business at Northwestern University.

My job was to organize different types of technology devices for professors during their lectures. This included remote clickers for slideshow presentations, handheld microphones, etc. I would prep the devices, deliver them to the classrooms, get derided by MBA students, and then leave. I had this job for six months which was longest of the dark times. It was consistent work, a massive increase of pay from $8.25 to $9 an hour, and provided leftover food for lunch. Win, win, win. I spent all of my money on rent and bills, so around Christmas, I had no money for gifts for anyone in my family. A few days after all the students left for the holidays, they dumped a pile of free XXXL sweatshirts and sweatpants on a table that went untouched because nobody wanted them. Or so they thought.

Christmas morning at my house is intense. There are seven people in my immediate family; and then adding in significant others, nieces, and nephews, it's like the opening scene from *Home Alone*. Our tradition is for each person to open their gifts individually. It takes roughly three to four hours for everyone to finish opening presents. This Christmas morning was different because each of my family members were getting something special from me this year. My sister Anna—who is five feet, two inches and very tiny—opened her gift from me to find a nice XXXL Kellogg School of Business sweatshirt.

"Oh, nice. Thank you, John."

Hours later, my sister Maria opened my gift which was a cozy XXXL Kellogg School of Business sweatshirt.

"Okay, thanks, John."

Every person in my family, including significant others, got an XXXL sweatshirt courtesy of Northwestern University. How did Santa know that everyone wanted an XXXL Kellogg School of Business sweatshirt? It was truly a Christmas miracle.

I left my job at Northwestern because I received a job offer for an office manager position that paid $40,000 a year, which was the equivalent of winning the lottery. It was a small luxury bedding company run by a Greek family that specialized in high-thread-count sheets that were made in China. Clearly sounds like a stable job and company that definitely won't go out of business in less than a year. I'm in!

Their office was even smaller than the MacBook repair office. Only one person and a plant could fit inside. My initial two duties were to set up the office furniture and then the office phone. I worked there for a total of one month. The first three weeks were moving in furniture—carrying tables, desks, and chairs. I put up company banners and work plaques with sayings like "If opportunity doesn't knock, build a door." In my final week, I had everything set up and ready to take calls. I received three calls on that phone. The first one was a wrong number. The second call was my boss's daughter verifying that the phone worked. The third call was my boss telling me that they had to let me go because they could not afford my salary.

Why didn't any of my employers realize that even start-up companies had to pay their employees!? Every time I was let go, they sounded surprised like

"I had no idea I had to pay you!" The job description for this position should've been "Seeking human who can lift heavy things, use a phone, and cope with bad news."

This job ended just as my one-year lease was expiring, and considering how my life was going, I thought it would be wise not to renew. I had no money and no place to live, but I didn't want to go back living with my parents. (Again, see chapter 6). I decided to crash at my cousin's apartment, which he shared with four other guys who were super into UFC, drinking, and EDM. There were strange people coming in and out of their place all the time. It was not the ideal place to stay because there wasn't any extra room and mainly because nobody wanted me there. I slept on a pile of my cousin's clothes in the corner of his room. This went on for a month until my spine started to curve inward. One of the roommates would sleep over at his girlfriend's house at least five nights a week, so there was an open bed. Now, he was very explicit about people not sleeping in his bed, especially people who weren't paying rent and secretly wearing his belts. When he was gone, I didn't hesitate to hop in his bed and snuggle up to the sensual sounds of EDM blasting from the other room.

At this time, I was working at a small social media company as a copywriter. It was an agency, so I was working extremely late hours. Not really enjoying it, but it provided me with portfolio materials that I would later leverage for a better job. I was dating this girl at the time who I met on an online dating app. Claire was an extremely kind and generous person, but I didn't see a future with her. She saw where I was living and correctly assumed her place was better suited for us to hang out. I spent a lot of time there, so much so that she gave me her extra set of keys. We dated for a few months, but I was planning on ending our relationship soon. I had planned to break up with her on Friday after I came home from work.

During work that day, I got a call from my cousin telling me that his friend found out I was sleeping in his bed and kicked me out of the apartment. Hours later, I was called into HR and told I had been laid off from my freelance copywriter position. Having heard this so many times, I just left her office as she was still speaking because I had some important decisions to make. I was not going to move back in with my parents. Instead of breaking up with Claire, I was going to stay at her apartment for as long as I possibly could. I was able to live there for an additional three weeks straight without her knowing I didn't have a job or a place to live.

She lived close to my work and would drop me off and pick me up. Obviously, I feel terrible about this now, but at the time, it didn't even occur to me that I was doing something wrong. When you're in survival mode, morals are an afterthought. It's not a great place to be.

To keep up the ruse, I had to get ready for work every morning to go to a job I did not have anymore just so she could drop me off. Once I got to work, I would very slowly walk to the door and wait until she left. My old coworkers were always confused to see me every morning, thinking, *That guy still works here?* I would spend most of the day applying for jobs at a nearby coffee shop or, sometimes, walk back to her apartment and hang out there. I was deathly afraid that she would come home to find me in her apartment at 1:00 p.m. in the afternoon. After a while, it was clear she wanted me out of her place, but because I was in survival mode, I was going to make her kick me out. She never did. I've told this story to friends who've said, "She had to have known you didn't have anywhere to go!" It's possible, but I only cared that I could stay there. Things got awkward toward the end. I'm pretty sure she started making up fake business trips, likely thinking I would, of course, vacate the apartment in her absence.

"So I have a conference in Denver next week. I'll be gone Monday through Wednesday," Claire said.

"Cool, have a good trip! I hold down the fort here," I replied.

Miraculously, all of these business trips got cancelled at that last minute. She clearly didn't know who she was dealing with. As soon as I got another job, I found an apartment and broke up with her. She took it really well.

Lifestyle

*I love a good nap. Sometimes it's the only thing
getting me out of bed in the morning.*

NOTHING LASTS FOREVER, and thank goodness
because the dark times eventually came to an end. I
had been put through the wringer and accumulated
several bruises to my ego and my face. My next job
was a customer service rep for a snow removal company that I worked at for three months until they had
to start paying benefits and let me go. After that, I
started searching for workplaces that employed a lot
of women because I found the working conditions
were usually much better. If you find yourself at a
company that employs mostly young men, run!

In 2009, I was a student taking writing classes at
the Second City in Chicago. I had just read an article
about how the golf industry was taking a financial hit

because it is seen as a luxury. I was curious and asked my improv teacher if they had been affected by the recession and had seen a reduction in the number of students taking comedy classes.

"On the contrary," he said, "we're booming."

He explained the people who had lost everything decided to put any money they had left into doing something they always wanted to do.

If circumstances don't line up or you're not ready, you wind up with a job instead of a career. That's clearly what kept happening to me. I was working until 11:00 p.m. using creative brain power trying to come up with fun insurance tweets or did-you-know facts about medical devices. I'm sorry if you fell asleep during that sentence, I almost did as I was writing it. But that job led to another job that led to another one, and suddenly you pick your head up and you've been working in a field for ten years that you have absolutely no passion for.

To find a career, you first have to discover what you like and what you're good at. Some people are really good at certain things but hate doing them, which doesn't work. I met so many ex-lawyers doing comedy. It all depends on what you care about. If you want a job to provide for your family and have a nice life, that's great! I saw my dad work himself to the bone throughout my childhood. He drove three hours every day for eleven years so his kids could live in a nice area with a good school system. He's been extremely successful in corporate America, but he grew up as one of seven kids who did not have a lot of money. He made a conscious choice to do well to ensure that his family would never have to worry about money. He succeeded, but he paid a price for it. We sometimes ate dinner at almost nine o'clock waiting for him to come home. There were countless times where he would fall asleep on the couch in his suit as he was trying to loosen his tie. I knew at age fourteen that I was not taking that path. I never cared about money; I cared about doing work that was fulfilling. Yes, millennial. See chapter 5.

I wanted a career but always blamed my jobs for not having one. I enjoy writing and making people laugh and have been through two major recessions in just under thirty-three years. So I thought to myself, *Maybe writing a humorous self-help book would be fun, hard work, and satisfying.* You have to be honest with yourself about what you really want and what will make you happy. I thought I was okay with just having a job, but I'm clearly not. I wanted a career. Improv is a hobby, marketing is a job, and maybe writing can be my career. (Please tell your friends and enemies about this book.)

What I do know for sure is that I've spent infinitely more time and effort working at things I love for no money than I have for jobs that paid me. I worked much harder on a comedy sketch about two dogs trying to make out with each other than I ever did on a marketing campaign. If you find yourself putting a lot of time and effort into something you enjoy, don't be afraid to try and make it your career. You may fail, but then you'll know how to do it better next time. This recession and pandemic are the equivalent of hitting the restart button on your career. The 42 percent of the jobs lost are never coming back. You can be scared by that, or you can be liberated because you can try anything you want! If you're fifty-five years old and lost your job or perhaps the entire industry you worked in, try something you like. If not now, when?

It's easier for people to explain what they want versus what they need. We are often our worst enemies for knowing what is best for us. One of the best ways to figure out what you need is to actually get what you "wanted" and realize you're not satisfied. This happens in both the workplace and in relationships. When I was fully immersed in comedy, I was convinced I was going to be with a woman who was a huge movie and TV fan. I dreamt about dishing inside jokes back and forth to each other, only speaking in obscure movie lines. I started dating women in the comedy scene who were savants in this realm. There wouldn't be any debate on whether season 4 of *Mad Men* is the best or *The Social Network* is David Fincher's best work. Relax, *Fight Club* fans. I did this for the majority of my twenties, and what I discovered is that it just didn't work for me. I felt pressure to compete comedically, and it wasn't enjoyable. This was just my experience. There are countless numbers of comedy couples who are happy and have wonderful relationships. It just didn't work me. Now I'm happily married to a woman who has never seen *Back to the Future* and owns the DVD *Blue Crush*, which sits in my eclectic DVD collection despite my repeated attempts to destroy it.

In the workplace, it's common to chase titles and salaries. Those are two of the main bargaining chips employers use to attract employees. A 2010 study by Princeton University researchers showed that, once a person reaches an annual salary of $75,000 a year, they don't experience an increase of happiness regardless of how much more money they make. If you're not in your dream career now, rather than chasing money or titles, chase a lifestyle. Even if you can't incorporate your hobbies into your job, you can at least have time for them in your life.

My ex-lawyer friends I met doing comedy told me they really enjoyed the law. They liked going to court, debating, and researching. They liked the work. What they didn't like was the seventy- to eighty-hour work weeks that their firms demanded of them. They didn't like buying inflatable beds when they had to sleep overnight in their office. They liked the work but not the lifestyle. When you love the work, the lifestyle almost doesn't matter. That's the difference. That's a career. Your actions will tell you what you're willing to work for. Pay attention to the things you labor over versus the things you do just enough not to get chastised. The little details you labor over are the things you really care about. *Seinfeld* is considered one of the greatest TV shows of all time, and one of the reasons was because of the writing. When asked about the key to the show's success, Seinfeld said, "The casting was quick. The editing was quick. Everything else was quick, but we labored over the writing."

Aristotle said, "Pleasure in the job puts perfection in the work." It is 100 percent true. I will never be great at a job in marketing. I can be very good, but I'll never be great because I don't love it. I never think about marketing when I'm not at work. It's possible to not love what you do but be good at it. Many people accomplish that every day. The best job I ever had didn't provide my highest salary during my marketing career. The work was incredibly boring. I had no passion or willingness to move up in the company. So how could it have been the happiest I have ever been in a job? Because it provided me the lifestyle I wanted. It was a job that allowed me to work remotely from Los Angeles, so I didn't need a car. I saved time with no commute. I was where I wanted to be which was close to the entertainment industry. I was able to afford improv classes and was even able to volunteer as an assistant baseball coach at a nearby high school. It afforded me the extra time to write comedy and sports articles that were later published. All my needs were being met. I was happy not because of my job but the lifestyle my job provided me. If the job provides you a lifestyle that allows you to do more of what you want, you figured it out. If you're thinking about what you want to do and aren't sure yet, that's okay. It takes a while to figure it out for some of us. I took me until I was thirty to find the lifestyle I needed. The way I discovered it was by doing many jobs that offered lifestyles I disliked.

Before COVID, I always had jobs that mandated me to be in the office. It drained my energy, made me lose focus on projects, and caused my soul to die at least once a week when I had to sign another coworker's birthday card.

Lifestyle offers you time to think. It allows you to step off the work treadmill for a bit and discover what you actually want. When you find yourself in a job that fits your background or skill set but doesn't coincide with your lifestyle, you'll never have adequate time nor be in an opportune mental state to try something new.

If you need money and are looking for a job you're not passionate about anyway, just find something you can for eight hours a day. If your dream career is being a chef but you find yourself working in IT, pick a job where you can leave at 5:00 p.m. every day rather than a more lucrative IT job that demands ten to twelve hours per day. The extra money won't make you happy, but a consistent schedule will provide you more time outside of work to cook. You'll be able to try new recipes in your spare time and cook for your friends. It's not about the type of job you'd like; it's "What can you do every day for eight hours a day?" Focus on what you can control versus what you can't. If you're at a job you hate, try to learn something that you can take with you. For me, it was these very real stories.

What this pandemic and recession shows is that the people at the top really don't know what they're doing, so if you can focus on something you like and are good at, there's no better time than now to showcase it.

Rejection

*What am I scared of? I'm scared of the
same thing that you are, everything.*

REJECTION EMAILS ARE deflating, especially when
you're constantly receiving notifications throughout
the day on your phone. It feels like the universe is
reminding you that you're not good enough. Updating
your résumé is annoying. Applying for countless jobs
is time consuming. Going on first, second, third, and
even fourth interviews can be exhausting. Spending
hours working on a project to submit for a job appli-
cation is awful because it could be a complete waste
of time if you don't end up getting the job. Answering
interview questions that begin with "Tell me about a
time when you…?" You get it.

The job search process is soul sucking, and you
need to make sure you're taking care of your mental

health, which is not something most companies prioritize. Mental health can be connecting with friends or family, exercising, or anything that takes your mind off what is worrying you. I've seen a therapist for the past four years, but I should have been seeing one for the past ten. Anxiety runs in my family, and I got a little bit of it. I don't take medication, but I do go to therapy which helps quell my anxiety that flares up particularly in the workplace. I've lost so many jobs in my career, and I'm always worried about losing another one. I used to worry when other people would be looking at my LinkedIn profile because I thought they were trying to sabotage me. It seems silly and irrational, but that's what anxiety is.

I made the mistake of comparing myself to where other people were in their careers. I would see LinkedIn updates of a person I used to work with become a director when I was still a coordinator. I would see a person who was doing comedy for a shorter time than me get an audition that I didn't get. Comparing yourself to others isn't helpful to your progress; it only hinders it and makes you feel worse.

Stop looking to the outside world for approval. If a company sends you a rejection email, who cares? That feeling of rejection is fleeting. Keep swinging and don't be afraid to fail. I used to create a safety net by making excuses for things not working out even before they happened. It was simply fear.

When we realize what we are meant to do, things just start happening. I knew I wanted to write this book for the last ten years, but I didn't because I was scared of what people would think of me. I was afraid to say that I wanted to be a writer because, if I committed to it, it might not work out. Don't waste years of your life not doing something you want just because you're afraid of what others might think.

Being jealous of someone who gets something you want is normal. Pay attention to it. Don't feel ashamed; it's a way of learning what you really want. Be happy for them, and remember, someone else's success isn't your failure. Honor others for their greatness, and then search inside yourself to find yours. Check in with yourself periodically throughout your working career and truly ask, "Am I happy right now?"

Negative thoughts are going to come regardless of what happens. It's life. The storm doesn't stay away forever. I had to learn how to first weather the storm so I could navigate myself through it. Don't worry about knowing all the answers, just show up for the test. It will get easier the more times you take it. Nobody aces it the first time around. The comedy writer and director Judd Apatow was asked in an interview why he always makes movies about losers, misfits, and people not fitting in. He responded, "Because how many people can really relate to Brad Pitt?"

About the Author

JOHN LALOGGIA IS a graduate of the Second City Writing Program and has a master's in communication from the University of Missouri–St. Louis. He lives in Chicago with his wife, Alexandra; son; and dog.

CPSIA information can be obtained
at www.ICGtesting.com
Printed in the USA
LVHW022356210621
690829LV00006B/243

9 781636 926766